Kissed by the Stars

Written by Brenda Arce
Illustrated by Naomi Fantauzzi

"Mami, tengo miedo,"
Marta whispered. "Why must we leave?"
"Don't worry, mi amor," her mami replied gently.
"Close your eyes. When you open them,
our new life begins."
Marta stared at the stars, hoping for a
shooting star. She knew her wish: for her family
to be safe on this new adventure.

"Mami, tengo miedo," susurró Marta.
"¿Por qué tenemos que irnos?"
"No te preocupes, mi amor," respondió su mamá
con suavidad. "Cierra los ojos. Cuando
los abras, nuestra nueva vida comenzará."
Marta miró las estrellas, deseando ver una fugaz.
Sabía cuál sería su deseo: que su familia
estuviera segura en esta nueva aventura.

As they stepped into their friend's apartment, she smiled warmly. "Welcome! I've prepared a room for you." Marta's mother set down their small bags, as it was all they could bring.

Al llegar al apartamento de su amiga, la mujer las recibió con una sonrisa cálida. "¡Bienvenidas! He preparado una habitación para ustedes." La madre de Marta dejó las pequeñas bolsas en el suelo; era todo lo que habían podido traer.

"Don't worry; everything will be fine. There's a school nearby," their friend added. Marta clutched her stuffed cat, holding it as if it were a piece of the home she had just left behind.

"No se preocupen; todo estará bien. Hay una escuela cerca," añadió su amiga. Marta abrazó con fuerza a su gatito de peluche, aferrándose a él como si fuera un pedacito del hogar que acababan de dejar atrás.

It had been a few weeks since Marta started school. She had been a good student back home, but here everything felt much harder. Understanding the subjects was difficult. Everything felt like a puzzle in her head, with pieces that didn't quite fit together.

Habían pasado algunas semanas desde que Marta empezó en su nueva escuela. En su país siempre había sido una buena estudiante, pero aquí todo le resultaba mucho más difícil. Entender las materias era complicado. Todo se sentía como un rompecabezas con piezas que no terminaban de encajar.

Her new home felt lonely. Marta missed her life back in Cuba. Although people seemed kind here, she was always afraid of saying something wrong. She whispered to herself, "Eres fuerte, tú puedes." (You are strong, you can do this.)

Su nuevo hogar también se sentía solitario. Marta extrañaba su vida en Cuba. Aunque la gente parecía amable, le daba miedo decir algo incorrecto. Se susurró a sí misma: "Eres fuerte, tú puedes."

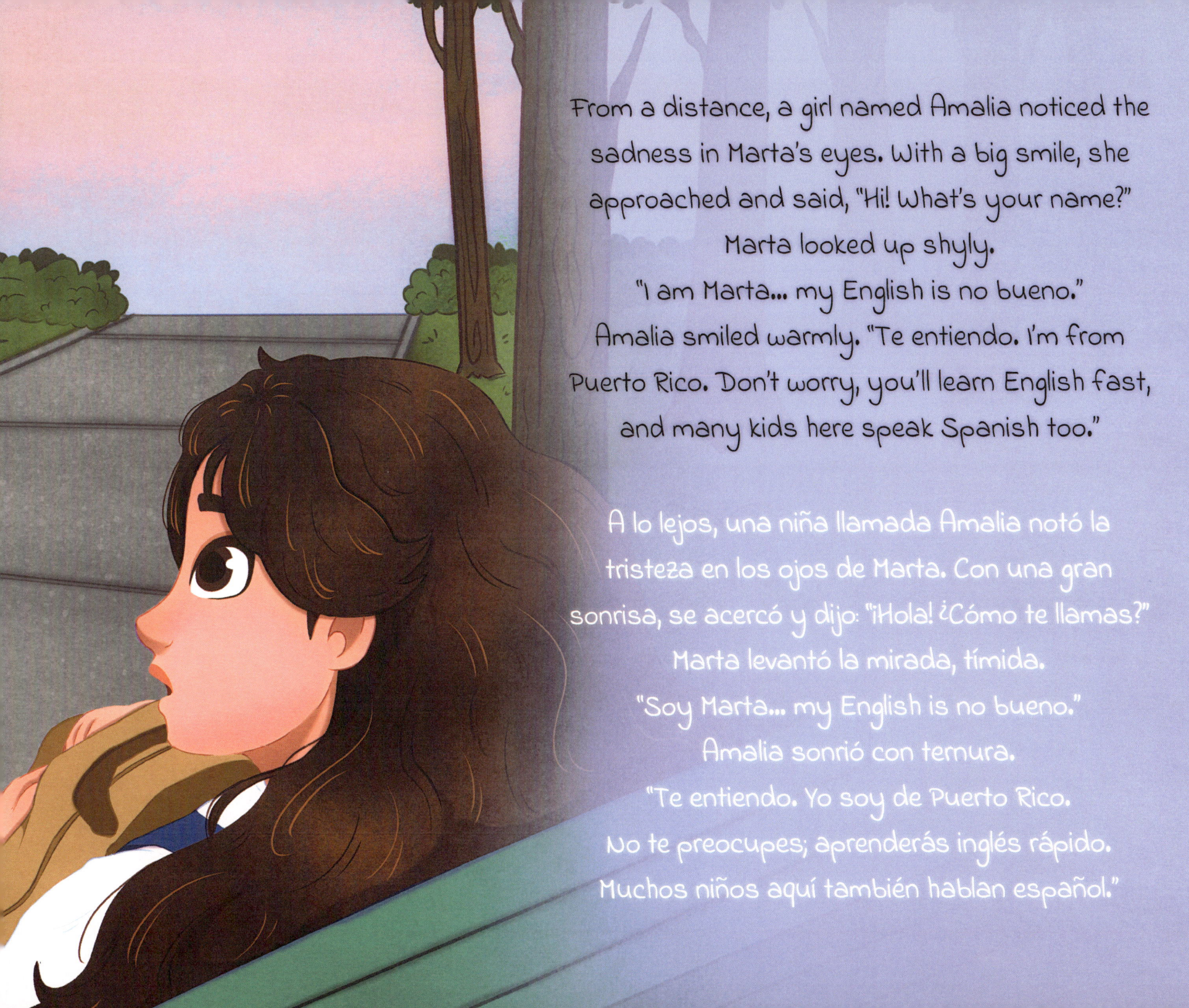

From a distance, a girl named Amalia noticed the sadness in Marta's eyes. With a big smile, she approached and said, "Hi! What's your name?"
Marta looked up shyly.
"I am Marta... my English is no bueno."
Amalia smiled warmly. "Te entiendo. I'm from Puerto Rico. Don't worry, you'll learn English fast, and many kids here speak Spanish too."

A lo lejos, una niña llamada Amalia notó la tristeza en los ojos de Marta. Con una gran sonrisa, se acercó y dijo: "¡Hola! ¿Cómo te llamas?"
Marta levantó la mirada, tímida.
"Soy Marta... my English is no bueno."
Amalia sonrió con ternura.
"Te entiendo. Yo soy de Puerto Rico. No te preocupes; aprenderás inglés rápido. Muchos niños aquí también hablan español."

At home, Amalia told her dad, "Papi, there's a new girl at school. She's from Cuba and looked so sad." Her dad smiled. "I know how that feels. Do you remember when you were new?"

Esa tarde, en casa, Amalia le dijo a su papá: "Papi, hay una niña nueva en la escuela. Es de Cuba y se ve muy triste." Su papá asintió con una sonrisa. "Sé cómo se siente. ¿Recuerdas cuando tú también eras nueva?"

Amalia nodded. Her family had moved a lot in the Army, but they always brought their favorite things. Suddenly, Amalia had an idea. She wanted to help. She wanted to make a difference.

Amalia lo recordó. Su familia se había mudado muchas veces por el trabajo en el Ejército, pero siempre llevaban consigo sus cosas favoritas. De pronto, a Amalia se le ocurrió una idea. Quería ayudar. Quería hacer una diferencia.

The next day, Amalia couldn't wait to see her friends and tell them about Marta. Her friends were all special and from different places!

Al día siguiente, Amalia no podía esperar para ver a sus amigas y contarles sobre Marta. ¡Todas eran especiales y venían de lugares diferentes!

Isa was from Argentina. She loved math and played video games. Carmen was from Ecuador and had a cool style. Claudia was from Colombia and was always so positive. Annia was from Mexico and loved making plans.

Isa era de Argentina y le encantaban las matemáticas y los videojuegos. Carmen era de Ecuador y tenía un estilo genial. Claudia era de Colombia y siempre estaba positiva. Annia era de México y le encantaba hacer planes.

"I met the new girl Marta," Amalia said. "She's Latina, like us! She's having a hard time. Can we help her?" "Yes!" everyone shouted. "We can have a bake sale!" said Isa.

"Conocí a la niña nueva Marta," dijo Amalia. "¡Es latina, como nosotras! La está pasando mal. ¿Podemos ayudarla?" "¡Sí!" gritaron todas. "¡Podemos hacer una venta de pasteles!" dijo Isa.

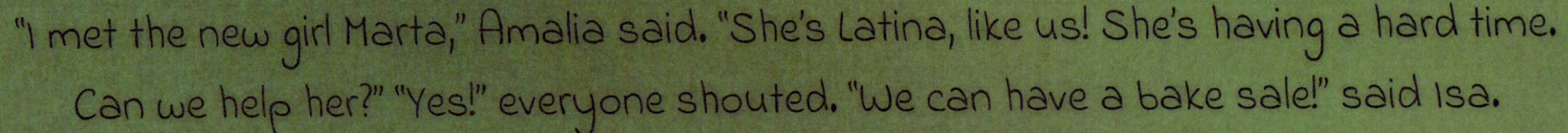

""Perfect! We can each make something from our countries," said Carmen.
"And we can find other ways to make her feel welcome," added Claudia.

"¡Perfecto! Cada una puede preparar algo típico de su país," añadió Carmen.
"Y también podemos buscar otras formas de hacerla sentir bienvenida," agregó Claudia.

Over the next few weeks, the girls worked together to help Marta. They went through their closets, choosing clothes she might like and find useful.

Durante las siguientes semanas, las niñas trabajaron juntas para apoyar a Marta. Revisaron sus clósets, eligiendo ropa que pudiera gustarle y serle útil.

"You would look amazing in the this," said Carmen with a bright smile. She loved clothes and wanted to share pieces that were special to her.

"¡Te verás increíble con esto!" exclamó Carmen con una gran sonrisa. Le encantaba la ropa y quería compartir prendas especiales para ella.

They invited Marta to do schoolwork at their houses. "That's correct!" said Isa. "You're learning English so fast."

Invitaron a Marta a hacer la tarea en sus casas. "¡Eso está correcto!" dijo Isa. "Estás aprendiendo inglés muy rápido."

Marta held up her stuffed cat. "This is Pelusa. I love her because she was a gift from my grandmother."
"She's adorable," Isa replied.

Marta levantó a su gatito de peluche. "Esta es Pelusa. La quiero mucho porque fue un regalo de mi abuela."
"Es adorable," respondió Isa.

They included her in fun activities and playdates. "Isn't the playground so pretty today?"

Las niñas la incluían en juegos y actividades divertidas. "¡Qué bonito está el parque hoy!"

"Look at the flowers!
They are like little pieces of sunshine,"
Claudia said, twirling happily.
"The world is so wonderful," she added.

"¡Mira las flores,
parecen pequeños rayos de sol!"
dijo Claudia, dando vueltas felizmente.
"El mundo es maravilloso," añadió.

As the girls continued helping Marta adjust to her new school, Annia kept a close eye on the bake sale preparations.

Mientras las amigas ayudaban a Marta a adaptarse a su nueva escuela, Annia se encargaba de los preparativos para la venta.

"These flyers look amazing!" Amalia exclaimed, holding one up.
Annia replied with a proud smile. "My mom helped me put them all around the neighborhood."

"¡Estos volantes se ven increíbles!" exclamó Amalia, sosteniendo uno.
Annia sonrió con orgullo. "Mi mamá me ayudó a ponerlos por todo el vecindario."

At home, Amalia helped Abuela Fela.
The warm smell of pasteles filled the kitchen.
"How many should we make?" asked Amalia.

En casa, Amalia ayudaba a la Abuela Fela.
El aroma de los pasteles llenaba la cocina.
"¿Cuántos debemos hacer?" preguntó Amalia.

"Enough to feed the whole world!" joked Abuela Fela. "But maybe we start with two dozen." Amalia laughed. "Let's do three dozen, just to be safe." The more they sold, the more they could help Marta.

"¡Suficientes para alimentar al mundo entero!" bromeó la abuela. "Pero mejor empecemos con dos docenas." Amalia se rió. "Hagamos tres docenas, por si acaso." Cuantos más vendieran, más podrían ayudar a Marta.

Amalia sold Puerto Rican pasteles, Isa brought Argentine empanadas, Carmen shared Ecuadorian bolas de yuca, Annia made Mexican tamales, and Claudia wowed everyone with Colombian pan de bono. They raised money for Marta and shared a little piece of their cultures with the neighborhood.

Amalia vendió pasteles puertorriqueños. Isa trajo empanadas argentinas. Carmen compartió bolas de yuca ecuatorianas. Annia preparó tamales mexicanos. Y Claudia sorprendió a todos con pan de bono colombiano. Recaudaron dinero para Marta y compartieron un pedacito de sus culturas con la comunidad.

A man walking by said, "This is wonderful, niñas. My family came here from Venezuela many years ago, and I know how hard it can be to start over. Keep doing what you're doing; you're making a difference."

Un hombre que pasaba se detuvo y dijo: "Esto es maravilloso, niñas. Mi familia vino de Venezuela hace muchos años, y sé lo difícil que puede ser empezar de nuevo. Sigan haciendo lo que están haciendo; están haciendo una diferencia."

The girls went to Marta's house with a big surprise. When Marta and her mom opened the door, they were amazed at everything the girls had brought. "I don't know what to say," her mom said, her voice shaking. "You've already been so kind to Marta." Amalia smiled. "¡Unidas somos más!"
(Together we are stronger.)

Las niñas fueron a la casa de Marta con una gran sorpresa. Cuando ella y su mamá abrieron la puerta, se quedaron sin palabras. "No sé qué decir," dijo la madre de Marta, con la voz temblorosa. "Ya han sido tan amables con Marta" Amalia sonrió. "¡Unidas somos más!"

"I am so lucky!" said Marta. "We are the lucky ones!" shouted the girls.
And so continued a beautiful journey of friendship.

"¡Qué afortunada soy!" dijo Marta. "¡Nosotras somos las afortunadas!" gritaron las niñas. Y así continuó un hermoso viaje de amistad.

That night, Marta lay in bed, gazing at the stars.
They reminded her of the night she left Cuba, when she wished upon a shooting star.

Esa noche, Marta se acostó mirando las estrellas.
Le recordaban la noche en que dejó Cuba, cuando pidió una estrella fugaz.

A soft smile appeared on her face.
"Now I know... my lucky star was never in the sky. They were my friends all along."

Una suave sonrisa apareció en su rostro. "Ahora sé... que mi estrella de la suerte no estaba en el cielo. Eran mis amigas todo este tiempo."

Brenda Arce - Author

Brenda Arce is an award-winning children's author and advocate for diversity. Her debut picture book, Kissed by the Sun, earned multiple honors at the 2024 International Latino Book Awards, including Best First Children's Book and Most Inspirational Children's Picture Book, as well as the 2025 Emerging Author Award from Best Sellers Choice. Her second book, Kissed by the Stars, continues her mission to celebrate culture, empathy, and the power of community through a heartwarming story of friendship and resilience.

Beyond her work as an author, Brenda is a respected business leader with nearly two decades of experience in the staffing industry, where she connects talented professionals with exceptional companies.

Brenda is also a passionate advocate for women's empowerment. As Vice President of TheLatinaPro®, she helps create spaces where Latinas can grow, lead, and build meaningful connections. Guided by the motto "Unidas somos más," she supports initiatives that uplift women across generations and industries.

Inspired by her Puerto Rican roots and her son, Joshua, Brenda uses her voice to champion belonging, representation, honoring one's story, and the importance of kindness toward others.

Acknowledgement

I am the lucky one!

To my family, Sebastian & Matthew and my friends, who have crossed my path and, in their own ways, shaped my journey. To Claudia, a special girl who left us far too soon yet always saw the best in the world, and to her mother, my friend Glorisel, your strength continues to inspire me. This book is inspired by the brave women who experience loss, change and new beginnings. Most of all, to my son Joshua. You are my guiding star, and my greatest hope is that you grow up brave, compassionate, and full of light.

Text Copyright © 2025 by Brenda Arce
Illustrations Copyright © 2025 by Naomi Fantauzzi

All rights reserved. No part of this book may be reproduced or transmitted in any form or by any means, electronic or mechanical, including photocopying, recording, or by any information storage and retrieval system, without written permission from the publisher, except for brief quotations used in reviews or scholarly works.

For permissions, contact: www.kissedbythesun.org

First Edition: Miami, FL
Printed in Miami, FL
ISBN: 979-8-9853149-3-9

www.ingramcontent.com/pod-product-compliance
Ingram Content Group UK Ltd.
Pitfield, Milton Keynes, MK11 3LW, UK
UKRC050305240426
12049UKWH00015B/165